Withdrawn

THE IVORY COAST

pictures

VISUAL
GEOGRAPHY
SERIES

by Albert Rosellini

S STERLING PUBLISHING CO., INC. NEW YORK

Oak Tree Press Co., Ltd. London & Sydney

VISUAL GEOGRAPHY SERIES

Afghanistan	Fiji	Jamaica	Puerto Rico
Alaska	Finland	Japan	Rhodesia
Argentina	France	Jordan	Rumania
Australia	French Guiana	Kenya	Russia
Austria	Ghana	Korea	Saudi Arabia
Belgium and Luxembourg	Greece	Kuwait	Scotland
Berlin—East and West	Greenland	Lebanon	Senegal
Bolivia	Guatemala	Liberia	South Africa
Brazil	Guyana	Madagascar (Malagasy)	Spain
Bulgaria	Haiti	Malawi	The Sudan
Canada	Hawaii	Malaysia and Singapore	Surinam
The Caribbean (English-	Holland	Mexico	Sweden
Speaking Islands)	Honduras	Morocco	Switzerland
Ceylon (Sri Lanka)	Hong Kong	Nepal	Tahiti and the
Chile	Hungary	New Zealand	French Islands of
China	Iceland	Nicaragua	the Pacific
Colombia	India	Nigeria	Taiwan
Costa Rica	Indonesia	Norway	Tanzania
Cuba	Iran	Pakistan and Bangladesh	Thailand
Czechoslovakia	Iraq	Panama and the Canal	Tunisia
Denmark	Ireland	Zone	Turkey
Dominican Republic	Islands of the	Paraguay	Uruguay
Ecuador	Mediterranean	Peru	The U.S.A.
Egypt	Israel	The Philippines	Venezuela
El Salvador	Italy	Poland	Wales
England	Ivory Coast	Portugal	West Germany
Ethiopia			Yugoslavia

j 966.5
ROS

—M— 3/77 Pub. 339

The publishers wish to thank the following for the use of the photographs in this book: Fraternité Matin; Photivoire; Photo Information of Ivory Coast; Albert Rosellini; United Nations.

Copyright © 1976 by Sterling Publishing Co., Inc.
419 Park Avenue South, New York, N.Y. 10016
Distributed in Australia and New Zealand by Oak Tree Press Co., Ltd.,
P.O. Box J34, Brickfield Hill, Sydney 2000, N.S.W.
Distributed in the United Kingdom and elsewhere in the British Commonwealth
by Ward Lock Ltd., 116 Baker Street, London W 1
Manufactured in the United States of America
All rights reserved

Library of Congress Catalog Card No.: 76–19802
Sterling ISBN 0-8069-1214-6 Trade   Oak Tree 7061-2517-7
1215–4 Library

Armed with a sharp-pointed stick, a watchman stands guard at the Bouaké Dam.

CONTENTS

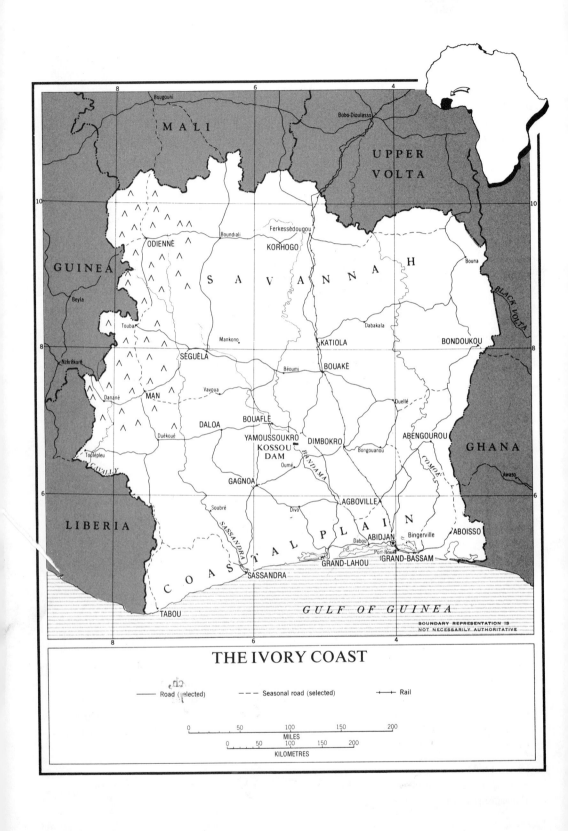

THE IVORY COAST

—— Road (selected) - - - Seasonal road (selected) +—+— Rail

0   50   100   150   200
MILES
0   50   100   150   200
KILOMETRES

The thrusting rock formation, "Tooth of Man," is a familiar landmark in the mountainous region of Man.

I. THE LAND

THE IVORY COAST is a roughly square-shaped land on the Atlantic seaboard of West Africa. With an area of about 124,000 square miles (322,000 sq. km.), the country is slightly larger than New Mexico or the British Isles.

The Ivory Coast is bounded on the south by 330 miles (528 km.) of Atlantic Coast. The other boundaries are formed by five adjacent nations—Liberia and Guinea on the west, Mali and Upper Volta on the north, and Ghana on the east.

The boundaries of the Ivory Coast were created by the Fren, who established a protectorate over this 1 of green forests and golden savannahs in 3. The country derived its name from the hu. herds of elephants and the ivory trade which flourished there at that time. Today, the elepi int population is greatly reduced, the ivory trad has been outlawed, and the once sleeping forests and savannahs are vibrating with economic activity.

The land is divided into three topographic

A mother carries her child outside their home in the village of Atiebouakro. Much of the family life takes place out-of-doors.

In 1973, the Ivory Coast exported 115,000 tons (126,500 tonnes) of pineapple. Over half the pineapples are processed and packed in local canneries.

zones, the plains, the plateaux, and the mountains, and two vegetative zones, the forest and the savannah.

THE PLAINS

The plains begin at the coastline, 330 miles (528 km.) of palm trees, sand and fiercely pounding surf. The regularity of the coast is interrupted by 100 miles (160 km.) of delicate, fingerlike lagoons which stretch to the east and west of Abidjan, the capital city.

From the coast, the low-lying, often swampy plains reach inland as far as Bouaké, 175 miles (280 km.) to the north.

The constant heat and humidity of the plains region maintain a thick, thriving tropical forest that covers the southern half of the country. Near Abidjan, the wet and green luxuriance of the forest is being encroached upon slowly, but steadily, by neat, symmetrical plantations of pineapples, bananas, and oil palms.

PLATEAUX

The plains slope gently, imperceptibly, upwards in a northerly direction, finally reaching an altitude of about 700 feet (210 metres). Here begins the northern area, a massive, inconsistent plateau occasionally spotted with mounds and hills.

This is the land of savannah, sparsely wooded grasslands that turn straw-brown during the long severe dry season, and green during the rains. The relatively dry climate here makes the land inhospitable to most large trees, but the baobab, which has the ability to store water in its trunk for long periods of time, is quite common.

MOUNTAINS

A ridge of highlands rises in the northwest between Man and Odienne. It is part of a vast ensemble of mountains and hills that has its midpoint in Guinea, and which peaks at the summit of Mt. Nimba, 5,775 feet (1,732 metres), located at the point where the Ivory Coast, Guinea and Liberia meet.

The region of Man presents a mountainous forested landscape that is highlighted by Mt. Tonkoui, 4,260 feet (1,278 metres), and the thrusting rock formation called "Dent de Man" ("dent" in French means "tooth" and also "jagged peak").

RIVERS

There are three main rivers in the Ivory Coast, the Bandama, the Sassandra, and the Comoe. They all have their source in the northern plateaux and run almost directly

Black savannah buffaloes populate the northern region, often travelling in herds of 20 or more.

The lake village of Tiegba, about 40 miles (64 km.) to the west of Abidjan, is being developed as a tourist attraction.

north to south, emptying into the lagoons and finally the Atlantic. None of them is navigable. The 594-mile (952-km.) flow of the longest river, the Bandama, is interrupted at Kossou by a recently built dam that promises to double the country's power supply and improve irrigation.

WILDLIFE

The savannahs and forests of the Ivory Coast are populated by a variety of animal and bird life, representing all the major African species except the giraffe, rhinoceros and gorilla.

Large herds of elephants roam the southwest forest region which also is home to the small red buffalo, a number of species of antelope and wild hog, leopards, hyenas, and a great variety of smaller animals. Hippos can often be seen taking a bath in the rivers of the south. Monkeys range throughout the country, but are especially abundant in the dense forests.

In the northwest Ivory Coast, stretching over 2,500,000 acres (1,000,000 hectares) of wooded savannah, lies the Comoe National Park, which is the haunt of elephants, antelopes, buffaloes, lions and leopards.

The lagoon region, because it offers so many different ecological niches, plays host to a variety of birds such as ducks, plovers, egrets, herons, and terns. Birds of the jungle, such as the parrot and the plaintain-eater or taraco, often have bright feathers. Besides these year-round winged residents, there is also a large population of migratory birds from Europe, who come south for the winter.

The king of the Ivorian reptiles is the crocodile which is frequently found in the streams. Green mambas, vipers, cobras, and pythons are a few common Ivorian snakes.

CLIMATE

The two distinct climatic regions of the Ivory Coast correspond to the topographic and vegetative zones.

The southern half of the country is characterized by a tropical climate—the temperature is constant at around 80°F. (27°C.) and the humidity is high. The land is drenched from April to June, the long rainy season, and again in October and November, the short rainy season. The rainstorms are brief but frequent and they unleash enormous quantities of water. In some places along the coast, particularly in the southwest and the southeast corners, the average rainfall reaches 80 inches (200 cm.).

The northern climate is much drier and has greater differences in temperature. There is only one rainy season in the north, from May to October, and the average yearly rainfall is 47 inches (117 cm.).

*In the guise of a road,
civilization makes its way
into the backwoods.*

VEGETATION

The lush forest zone produces a great variety of plants, from huge trees to shrubs, vines and herbs. Among the trees are giant dracaenas (related to the familiar house plants kept in Europe and America), the bombax or cotton-tree, climbing palms of the genus *Calamus*, oil palms, raffia palms, which yield a commercially valuable fibre, and many species that yield latex or natural rubber.

Elephants range throughout the country but are especially plentiful in the forested lowlands of the southwest.

Other native trees of commercial value are the kola tree, which yields cola nuts, and the native West African coffee tree, *Coffea liberica*, as well as the African mahogany and cedar. Oil palms and coconut palms are abundant along the coast, and orchids, ferns and aroids (plants of the philodendron type) not only cover the forest floor but grow profusely upon the trunks and limbs of trees.

NATURAL RESOURCES

Rich soil and an abundant water supply are the chief natural resources of the Ivory Coast. The only minerals extracted commercially are diamonds and manganese, in relatively small quantities. Surveys have established the possibility of mining iron ore, gold, bauxite, lithium and colombo-tantalite.

CITIES

The population of the Ivory Coast, which numbered 4,800,000 in 1976, is mostly rural. Abidjan, the capital, and Bouaké, are the only cities of 100,000 people or more, although cities under 50,000 are fairly numerous.

Clouds hang low over the mountains of Man.

ABIDJAN

At the turn of the century, the slender canoes of the Ebrie fishermen slipped through the glassy lagoon waters surrounding Abidjan, a peaceful fishing village then of perhaps 700 inhabitants.

Today, cargo ships and sleek passenger liners churn those same waters. A mélange of shining skyscrapers and modern buildings, grey and gleaming white, rise from the land and the

The Abidjan suburb of Adjamoy, although of ramshackle appearance, bristles with activity.

city thoroughfares, crammed with cars, taxis, and buses, divide them into neat blocks. Over 600,000 people of many nationalities, working, laughing, talking, arguing, and sleeping, daily breathe life into the young metropolis.

The evolution of the city began in 1898 when the French colonial administration designated Abidjan as the terminus of a railway line that would penetrate inland towards the River Niger. In 1934, Abidjan, because of its increased importance as a hub of communications, replaced nearby Bingerville as the capital of the territory. But the real boost to population growth and economic development came in 1951 with the opening of a deep-water port and the Vridi Canal, a deep-water channel connecting Abidjan with the open sea. Thousands of West Africans, drawn by the prospect of work and excitement, flocked to the city. Europeans and Lebanese were attracted by the possibilities of international commerce and a sound economic climate. The continuing wave of immigrants has made Abidjan a vibrant international port city, with an atmosphere of intrigue and sophistication, and promises to boost the total population to 700,000 by 1980.

Abidjan consists of five sections connected by super-highways and two bridges. One of these sections, called the Plateau, has graceful modern architecture rising above the lagoons, and boasts office buildings, elegant restaurants and boutiques, theatres, and a small population of European residents. The Plateau is the administrative and financial heart of the city and of the country. Cocody and Marcory, situated east of the Plateau, are the "quartiers de résidence aisée" or wealthy suburbs, attractive ensembles of villas and manicured gardens.

The great majority of the people are concentrated in the teeming African suburbs of Treichville and Adjame. Here life pulses and burns day and night with an excitement that

An aerial view of Abidjan shows the Pyramid Building at the right and the Hotel Ivoire across the lagoon in Cocody. The skyscraper at the left is a bank building.

can be best described in terms of the sounds that fill the air—laughter and argument, shouts of vendors and cries of children, the roar of crammed buses, loud "Afrobeat" music pouring out of countless record shops and night clubs. The residents, of whom half are Ivorians and half are other West Africans, live in ethnically distinct districts that maintain traditional ties and customs in the midst of a composite and changing society.

BOUAKÉ

Bouaké, 245 miles (392 km.) north of Abidjan, is situated in the middle of the country, on the southern edge of the savannah. A bustling agricultural and industrial town that spreads out rather than up, it is the site of the oldest and largest textile factory in the country. Here also are food processing plants and soap, cigarette, chemical and automobile industries. An impressive mosque bears witness to a large Muslim population, many of them descendants

Students chat on the grounds of the National Institute of the Arts in Abidjan. The Institute trains art teachers, artists, craftsmen and technicians.

Abidjan's lush residential suburb of Cocody, with its expansive palm-shaded lawns, is inhabited mainly by European professionals, business executives, and foreign service personnel.

of the Dioula traders who established Bouaké many years ago as a vital link in a major trading route. The total population is a little over 100,000.

MAN

Situated in the west, near the Liberian and Guinean borders, and tied to the north and middle of the country by 15 major roads, Man, with a population of 35,000, is the administrative and commercial capital of the western region.

Each morning before dawn, a mist rises over the surrounding hills and pours into the valley, finally settling over the city of Man. As the morning sets in the mist burns away, revealing the green mounains that make this region so picturesque.

Because of the area's natural beauty and considerable folklore—the traditional dances of the villages are stunning—the region of Man is gradually being developed as a tourist attraction.

The market-place at Man. Plantains (large green bananas) are a staple food in the southern Ivory Coast. As in most African markets, a great deal of bargaining usually takes place before an agreeable price is reached.

The Pyramid Building exemplifies the creative modern architecture that graces the city of Abidjan.

OTHER CITIES

Korhogo, the capital of the northern area, and Ferkessédougou are major towns of similar size, about 25,000, set in the savannah lands of the north. Both have predominantly Muslim populations and are seats of the Senoufo, the second largest ethnic group in the Ivory Coast.

Agricultural staples—groundnuts (peanuts), millet, sorghum, rice, and yams are grown in these regions, and Ferkessédougou with its new sugar cane plantations and refinery will soon become the sugar capital of the Ivory Coast.

Yamoussoukro, home town of the Ivorian President, Felix Houphouët-Boigny, is growing and modernizing with an energy that typifies all of the Ivory Coast. Just outside of town lies the President's plantation—a sprawling agricultural experiment on which every Ivorian crop is grown and where new possibilities are being explored.

Yamoussoukro is also the site of the elaborate assembly hall that houses the country's single political party, the "Parti Démocratique de Côte d'Ivoire" (Democratic Party of the Ivory Coast).

Daloa is a thriving city of 45,000 that lies in the midst of a flourishing agricultural region.

Two modern bridges in Abidjan (one of which is seen here) connect the Plateau to the residential district of Treichville.

Women in costume dance at a reception given for the President of Senegal, who was on an official visit to the Ivory Coast.

2. HISTORY

WHILE MUCH of West Africa was being ravaged and decimated by countless wars among competing African kingdoms, the thick forests of the Ivory Coast remained unscathed, wrapped in jungle mystery.

The endemic diseases carried by certain mosquitos and the dreaded tse-tse fly held the threat of death for even the hardiest of explorers. The impassably thick jungle vegetation, the difficult coastline, and the dangerous crashing surf were natural barriers that effectively closed off this part of the West African Coast until the 15th century.

While this natural isolation had its advantages—the Ivory Coast was only lightly exploited by the slave trade—it also accounts for the fact that we know very little of the early history of the country.

In the 16th century, the Senoufo, who are today the second largest ethnic group in the Ivory Coast, occupied a large portion of land that stretched from Sikasso, Mali, to Bouaké. Then from the northwest, the Malinke (more commonly known as Dioula) came in a wave, prodding and pressing the Senoufo southwards.

The Dioula were enthusiastic money-makers who were expert at hawking their products, mostly cola and cereals, as well as their religion, Islam. The Dioula, along with the Muslim faith, spread rapidly and effortlessly across the savannahs to Bondoukou, where they established a major trading route to the River Niger.

Guere masks are grotesque combinations of human features and frills. In the traditional ceremonies, the masks embody the power of the ancestors and are meant to intimidate the onlookers.

while the Baoulé crossed the River Comoe and settled in the middle of the country.

FRENCH INFLUENCE AND COLONIZATION

It is known that the Portuguese and other Europeans touched on the Ivory Coast as early as the 14th century. However, in 1637, the first known French visitors to the Ivory Coast landed at Assinie. They were five missionaries, three of whom contracted jungle fever and died almost immediately. For the next 200 years, few attempts were made to establish posts along the Ivory Coast. The French founded settlements at Grand Bassam and Assinie, but these lasted only a few years.

Then in 1842, the French Government launched a policy of intensive exploration of the West African coast with an eye to acquiring potentially rich territories. This policy led to negotiations with chieftains at Grand Bassam and Assinie which resulted in treaties benefitting both parties. The French would protect the villages and pay an annual tribute,

In the 17th and 18th centuries, two Akan peoples—the Agni and the Baoulé—poured into the Ivory Coast from what is today Ghana. The Angi settled around Bondoukou,

A Baoulé chieftain sits surrounded by his entourage.

An Ebrié elder sits among his village's fishing canoes.

while the Africans would do business only with the French and allow them to establish forts.

In 1893, the Ivory Coast became an autonomous colony headed by a French governor and administration. Captain Louis-Gustave Binger, the commanding military officer of the colony, began to establish inland posts and to define the borders more precisely. He also founded Bingerville.

SAMORY

Some resistance to colonization was inevitable, but the French military never anticipated the well-trained armies of the Malinke sovereign, Samory Touré.

In the years 1879–1898, Samory and his army raged through Guinea, Mali, Upper Volta, Ghana and the Ivory Coast, periodically depleting and embarrassing the French forces with a combination of fury and tactical brilliance.

At one point, Samory established his kingdom in the northern Ivory Coast between Odienné and Bouna, completely annihilating

and plundering such towns as Bouna and Kong.

In 1898, Samory tried to lead his army across the mountainous region of Man and into

This man is demonstrating the traditional method of weaving, which was in use long before the arrival of the French.

The leaders of this Wobe village in the western mountain region invite a visitor to share in some foutou, the national dish of the Ivory Coast. This particular village is very remote, accessible only by a small footpath. The people very rarely see a foreigner.

Guinea in the midst of the rainy season. In a short time the elements took their toll and Samory's army was reduced by half. He was captured on September 29, 1898, at Gueoule,

50 miles northwest of Man. "Only hunger defeated us," he said defiantly. Samory was exiled to Gabon, where he died in 1900.

PACIFICATION

Although historically labelled the pacification period, the early 1900's were in fact a time when African resentment was kindled and fanned. The natives of the newly formed colony were forced by Governor Gabriel Angoulevent and the colonial administration to meet certain quotas of local products. Opponents of this practice were quickly disarmed, penalized, and sometimes exiled.

The French Government encouraged European settlers, especially farmers, by offering them 5-year freehold grants for coffee and cocoa plantations. African farmers resented the preferential treatment given to the foreigners. The antagonism abated slightly in 1937, when the Government became more liberal and sympathetic to the needs of the Africans, allowing them for the first time to organize a trade union.

When France swung to the right during World War II under the pro-Nazi Vichy régime, the liberal movement in the Ivory Coast was purged and discrimination, segregation, and forced servitude were again sanctioned by the colonial administration.

The opening of the deep-water port at Abidjan in 1951, by establishing easy trade and communication routes, set the stage for the economic boom in the Ivory Coast.

The 60 ethnic groups of the Ivory Coast became united in a single reaction of discontent.

FELIX HOUPHOUËT-BOIGNY AND THE RISE TO INDEPENDENCE

In 1944, a Baoulé chief named Felix Houphouët-Boigny, along with other leading planters, organized the *Syndicat Agricole Africain* (SAA). This anti-Vichy organization sought to secure better premiums for African producers, to eliminate discriminatory practices benefitting European farmers, and to abolish forced work. Its leaders, in particular Houphouët-Boigny, became associated in the public eye with emancipation.

After World War II, the more liberal De Gaulle administration gave the Ivory Coast its first opportunity to present its political concerns in Paris. In 1945, Houphouët-Boigny, by then a shining symbol of hope and unity, was resoundingly elected representative to the French National Assembly.

The young Ivorian representative presented a bill to the First National Constituent Assembly "proposing the abolition of all forms of forced labor in overseas France." It passed and almost overnight Boigny became a mythical hero and the recipient of a lasting gratitude that would facilitate all his future political aims.

An alliance between the SAA and the organized supporters of Boigny resulted in the "Parti Démocratique de Côte d'Ivoire" (PDCI) which dominated the political scene and dictated the course of events leading to independence.

Between 1946 and 1950, opposition parties were encouraged by the colonial administration, which viewed the rapid advancement of the African cause with some uneasiness. As a result of this outside pressure, the PDCI became internally more solid. The party transformed itself into a military organism and continually harassed the colonial government. It was a time of conflict, civil disorders, and bad economic conditions and the PDCI was rapidly losing its popular support.

Houphouët-Boigny and the PDCI realized that the cost of militancy was too high and aimed for and achieved reconciliation with the colonial administration. Opposing groups co-operated or were absorbed. Prices soared, the economy shot forward and the PDCI once again enjoyed almost universal support.

Meanwhile Houphouët-Boigny, then president of the PDCI, was gaining power in the French National Assembly and in 1956 he became a full-fledged French Cabinet Minister, the first African ever to do so.

Armed with such political power, Boigny was able to secure preferential allocations of French aid to the Ivory Coast, and attract European business interests to the country. Boigny, who so ably harmonized French policy with the political and commercial growth of the Ivory Coast, came to be known as the father

President Houphouët-Boigny meets France's late President Charles de Gaulle in Paris. Houphouët-Boigny was the first African ever to become a full-fledged minister in the French government.

of the country and his party, the PDCI, became synonomous with the body politic.

Independence came peacefully in 1960. The occasion did not mark an end to close relations with France but rather an accelerated commercial exchange and political rapport between the two governments.

President Houphouët-Boigny, dressed in a traditional robe, addresses his countrymen. The President likes to cultivate his image as the wise and conscientious tribal chieftain presiding over the extended family of the Ivorian people.

The Ivory Coast Government promotes co-operatives, such as this grocery in Marcoy, where food is discounted from 15 to 60 per cent.

3. THE GOVERNMENT

THE NATIONAL ASSEMBLY of the Ivory Coast adopted a constitution on October 31, 1960, providing for a strong presidency, for a degree of separation between the executive and legislative branches, and for an independent judiciary. The document echoed the United States constitution by declaring as its fundamental principle "government for the people, by the people, and of the people."

Within the framework of these loosely defined principles a new form of government, strong, authoritarian, yet conscientious, has evolved in the Ivory Coast.

THE ONE-PARTY SYSTEM

Since its inception in 1946, the PDCI and its President, Felix Houphouët-Boigny, have dictated the course of government in the country. All 70 members of the National Assembly, all administrative heads, and practically all of the voting public belong to the party.

While, in theory, the constitution provides for a free election of the President and members of the National Assembly every 5 years by direct universal suffrage, in fact free choice is exercised only within very strict limits. The

This hotel in Bouaké is part of a government-backed project to expand tourist facilities in the Ivory Coast.

voter does not cast his ballot for an individual, but rather for a list of candidates prepared in advance by a governmental nominating committee. The list of candidates for the National Assembly is drawn up by the President and a few top advisors.

Although opposing lists may be submitted to the voters, they very rarely are, because the cost of doing so is prohibitively expensive ($500 U.S. per candidate, or roughly twice the average yearly income) and also because there is virtually no chance of beating the party list.

It is very unlikely, therefore, that another party would ever gain access to the National Assembly.

The massive power and universal approval that the PDCI enjoys can be traced back to its beginning in 1946. When the party was being formed it sought not to recruit individual members but rather whole villages at a time. Other villages of the same ethnic group were then incorporated into the party. A person became a party member not by individual choice but by virtue of the fact that he belonged

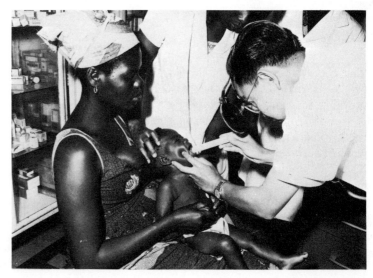

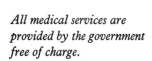

All medical services are provided by the government free of charge.

The Ivorian government, realizing that the future lies in the nation's young people, encourages youth participation in political affairs. Here a youth leader addresses a crowd.

This slender structure is the radio-communications tower in Bouaké. Communications in the Ivory Coast are quite good, with a government-controlled radio network that reaches 600,000 listeners, and a television system that reaches two thirds of the country.

to a particular ethnic group. This structure made it possible for the party to mobilize large amounts of support.

The movement spread quickly and soon the party embraced the great majority of ethnic groups in the Ivory Coast. The party and its already heroic leader, Houphouët-Boigny, came to be symbols of unity. The party rose in stature and power as the Ivorians came to believe that whosoever opposes the PDCI opposes unity.

PRESIDENT HOUPHOUËT-BOIGNY

Revered by the people, and filling a dual rôle as President of the PDCI and President of the Ivory Coast, Houphouët-Boigny possesses a degree of unquestioned, legitimized power that is rarely seen in democratic republics.

Major decisions, in any sphere of government, are not made without first consulting him. Usually, he and his cabinet officers are the initiators of legislation. While theoretically the National Assembly can veto the president's bills, in fact they have never done so.

Since becoming President in 1960, Boigny has almost single-handedly directed the policy of the Ivory Coast according to a far-sighted plan that is primarily geared towards material wealth. With an energetic and prosperous economy, Boigny believes, other domestic

23

President Houphouët-Boigny (first row, middle) poses with his cabinet.

matters, such as health and education, can be dealt with more quickly and effectively. Without a developed economy, they cannot be dealt with at all according to Boigny.

The first prerequisite to increased production and economic wealth is a peaceful and unified populace and Boigny will take whatever measures are necessary—occasionally violent or extra-legal—in order to ensure this kind of stability.

Boigny's philosophy of government can be likened to the attitude a parent might have towards raising a child. At lower levels of development, there is a need for more control and discipline. As the child matures, he or she is given more freedom and becomes increasingly self-directed.

The idea is reflected in Boigny's complete dominance of the political scene and the far-reaching power of his government. All communications are government operated and dispense a mild form of propaganda. There is no place for dissent in the Boigny régime. While Boigny always prefers to co-operate or appease dissenters by offering them high-ranking jobs or by engaging in lengthy, conciliatory "dialogues," he does not hesitate to use force when these methods fail.

The Government Technical Centre at Gagnoa trains instructors in handicrafts, woodworking, metal work and masonry.

This sculptor carving a mask out of a block of wood works at a government-sponsored craft shop near Abidjan.

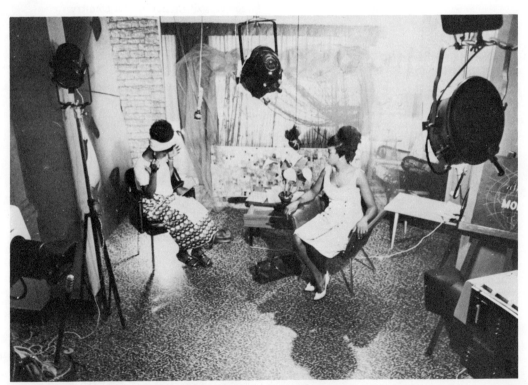

Ivorian women prepare for a television talk show. In 1970, there were an estimated 10,500 sets in the Ivory Coast. The government has subsidized an educational television network which reaches many villages, dispensing primary education, health education, news of agricultural developments and methods.

Boigny's greatest opposition in the past years has come from student organizations, which are critical of the one-party system, capitalism, limited freedom, or other aspects of the government. When an implacably hostile student organization instigated a strike at the University of Abidjan in May, 1969, Boigny ordered the army to occupy the university, and to arrest some 400 students. Most of them were released upon signing a pledge to refrain from further political activity unless under the auspices of the PDCI.

Outside of occasional ideological conflicts with students, there is little opposition to Boigny's policies. The majority of the population approves of the government and looks to Boigny as a traditional chieftain. Thus Boigny, utilizing all the power available to him, as well as his own consummate skill as a politician, has established peace and stability in the Ivory Coast. He has forged 60 different ethnic groups into a single energetic and progressive nation.

FOREIGN POLICY

The foreign policy of the Ivory Coast derives from Boigny's conviction that the foundation of a country's well-being is economic rather than political. In order to develop, to satisfy human needs, to become a strong nation, it is first necessary to build a sound economy. Political objectives, such as political freedom, or Pan-Africanism are a secondary consideration, important only insofar as they promote a healthy economy. Thus the foreign policy of the Ivory Coast always tends toward negotiation and conciliatory diplomacy, never toward conflict.

Boigny led the Ivory Coast to independence reluctantly, fearing that the country might lose the substantial amounts of financial aid that France bestowed on its overseas territories. As it turned out, independence has proved beneficial to the Ivory Coast, as the country now enjoys healthy, commercial interaction with France, but on a more equal footing.

The foreign policy of the Ivory Coast is successful to the extent that it makes friends, and more especially financial partners, of other countries. France, Italy, Germany, the United States, Japan, and Holland have all invested large sums of money in the country.

While the Ivory Coast is not as politically oriented as some nearby African nations, such as Guinea or Ghana, and thereby open to their criticism, its foreign policy has successfully created friendly relations that enable the countries to co-exist peacefully.

President Houphouët-Boigny turns the switch that will set the Kossou dam in operation.

This young Ivorian is carrying gourds filled with "bangui," or palm wine, the preferred drink of the Ivory Coast. The palm wine tapster makes an incision near the top of the tree and attaches a gourd, into which the sweet sap flows. The sap ferments in a couple of days and the result is bangui, a pungent, mildly alcoholic refresher.

4. THE PEOPLE

BEFORE THE COMING of the French, the land that is now the Ivory Coast was inhabited by 60 ethnic groups, each with a distinct language and customs. This human mosaic was formed by the juncture of four culture circles or civilizations, radically different from each other in terms of geographical origin, history, customs and language. Each of these culture circles had its midpoint outside of the Ivory Coast and therefore the groups often had more in common with the people of surrounding countries than

with their compatriots. These four groups are called the Atlantic East, the Atlantic West, the Voltaic and the Mandingo.

Only since the mid-1960's have the people, who now number 4,800,000, begun to develop a national consciousness—to consider themselves first of all, as Ivorians, and only secondarily as members of a particular ethnic group.

The social evolution that has taken place in the Ivory Coast—from a basically haphazard collection of 60 ethnic groups to a single nation

A mother relaxes in a rope hammock with two of her children.

with a sense of unity—represents one of the most dramatic social accomplishments in African history.

THE ATLANTIC EAST

The outstanding groups of this culture complex are the Agni and the Baoulé. Originally part of the Akan Kingdom in adjacent Ghana, these two groups separated and migrated east to the Ivory Coast 200 to 300 years ago. The Lagoon Cluster Peoples, also members of this complex, are comprised of scattered and isolated tribes living along the lagoon-dotted eastern shore.

AGNI

When the Agni separated from the Akan Monarchy and moved into the Ivory Coast, they brought with them the tradition of monarchy. They possessed an ingrained sense of the rightness of monarchy as a form of social organization. Thus, as they situated themselves in the eastern portion of the Ivory Coast between the River Comoe and the Ghanaian border, they established four kingdoms. One of these, the Sanwi Kingdom, had such a strong and irrepressible sense of cohesion that it attempted in 1959, to declare itself independent from the Ivory Coast.

The Agni are an intensely proud people, knowledgable in the traditions and history of their culture. The dignity of the people and the kingdom is symbolized by an elaborate golden stool that is possessed by each king.

BAOULE

According to legend, these people, originally residing in Ghana, were led by the wise and celebrated Queen Abra-Pokou. The Queen ordered that a surplus of cereals be stored up in case of famine. When famine did come, the people were attacked by ruthless enemies. Rather than forfeit the food, the Queen led her people east into the Ivory Coast. They reached the River Comoe, which they found impossible to cross. A sacrifice to the gods was necessary. Queen Abra-Pokou sacrificed her own child, the trees bent down across the river to form a bridge, and the queen led her people into a new land of safety and peace. Thus it is said that the word Baoulé means "the little one dies."

A witch doctor demonstrates courage and magical prowess by "swallowing" a snake.

The legend demonstrates a reverence for agriculture that persists today among the Baoulé, who have gained a reputation as the best farmers in the Ivory Coast.

LAGOON CLUSTER PEOPLES

The Lagoon Cluster peoples represent a tradition of sailing and fishing, although the modern economy has forced many of them to move inland and to engage in cash-crop farming

They migrated from the East earlier than the Agni and Baoulé and settled in scattered tribes. Although sharing many linguistic and cultural similarities, the tiny groups have little to do with each other.

Perhaps the best known group among the Lagoon Cluster peoples are the Ebrié of Abidjan who build their houses on stilts over the water, and who fish from slender canoes.

THE ATLANTIC WEST

The peoples of this culture complex inhabit the southwest forest region, and are probably the oldest residents of the Ivory Coast. For years their villages were wrapped in the

The houses of the Ebrié fishermen are built upon stilts.

29

impenetrable and mysterious forest, and some of these groups are known to have practiced cannibalism. The seclusion of these peoples was brought to an end around 1900 by the colonial government.

The southwest forest peoples do not have the fierce sense of cultural pride that inspires the Agni and Baoulé—they are not heirs to a high culture and they have arrived at their present location only through being pushed south by northern conquerors.

DAN

Also called Yacouba, this group inhabits the mountainous region of Man. Political power among the Dan is invested in the village chief, who is also frequently the leader of the secret

All Dan masks are remarkably consistent, having the same serene expression and concave profile. In this case, the eyes are encircled by metal rings.

The man with the tape recorder is the leader of this Wobe village. The people are fascinated by electronic gadgetry and the tape recorder, when it was played back, drew shrieks of excitement from the villagers.

A Senoufo funeral procession occurs after the spirit of the dead man has been exorcised by the frantic, communal beating of drums. After the corpse is buried, there are four days of mourning. The widow's head is shaved and she is kept in solitary confinement for 40 days.

society. The Dan are known for their acrobatic dances and masks.

OTHER GROUPS

The Bété, Guéré, and Oube or Wobé, together numbering over 300,000 are other major groups of the Atlantic West region.

VOLTAIC GROUP

The Voltaic culture complex extends across the northern Ivory Coast, northern Ghana, and Upper Volta. Its major representative in the Ivory Coast is the Senoufo group.

SENOUFO

The Senoufo came to the Ivory Coast from the Sudanic region in the 16th century and formed various tribes across the savannah, settling in Korhogo, Sequela, Odienné, and Kong.

Being a very peaceful and sedentary people by nature, concerned only with farming, the Senoufo were exploited and pushed back by more military-oriented groups. During the rampages of the Malinke sovereign, Samory Touré, whole Senoufo villages were annihilated.

The Senoufo now reside in the north-central Ivory Coast, principally around Korhogo and Ferkessédougou. The Senoufo feel a strong relationship for the land and their agrarian way of life and have a conservative attachment to peasant values—they are little affected by modern methods and little susceptible to change.

MANDINGO

It is believed that in the last several thousand years the Mandingo peoples have been responsible for two great empires, both of which were developed in what is today Mali.

The Mandingo culture complex could at one time be divided into three main groups—Malinke, Bambara, and Dioula—but it is no longer easy to distinguish them as their language and customs have become increasingly similar. In the Ivory Coast, all members of the Mandingo group are called Dioula.

DIOULA

The Dioula possess a cultural character that is very different from the other groups in the Ivory Coast. They are not attached to the soil. They cultivate without conviction and only of necessity, and are always on the lookout for a more profitable enterprise, even if it means uprooting themselves and settling in a strange land.

The Dioula reside mainly in the northwestern part of the Ivory Coast but many travel throughout the land in search of opportunity. Imbued with a religious conviction to match their business acumen, the Dioula account for all but a few of the over 1,000,000 Moslems in the Ivory Coast.

FOREIGNERS

Foreigners in the Ivory Coast number about 1,000,000 or one fifth of the total population. They are drawn to the Ivory Coast because, by African standards, it is a rich country. Many of them are of the Mossi tribe of Upper Volta. Because of their background of extreme poverty in the arid and barren region of Upper Volta, the Mossi are willing to work at any job and to accept the lowest pay. The jobs are available

These Senoufo musicians are playing balafons. The balafon is actually a wooden xylophone played with rubber mallets. Full and resonant sounds are created by the gourds that hang underneath the instrument.

Vine bridges like these are made in a single night by the secret societies of the Dan. The bridge is woven into hanging vines in a way that defies explanation. During the night of construction, the secret society does not allow anyone to come within a mile of the bridge, lest their secret be discovered.

Togolese and citizens of Benin (formerly called Dahomey) in the Ivory Coast.

Lebanese, who have long been in business in West Africa, are found in cities throughout the Ivory Coast operating grocery stores, hotels and restaurants. Europeans in the Ivory Coast number 50,000, most of them French, and the majority reside in the commercial hubs of Abidjan and Boulé. They are most frequently engaged in government services, missionary work, education, or commercial enterprise.

LANGUAGE

There are over 60 variations of the spoken word in the Ivory Coast. Agni, Baoulé, Senoufo, and Dioula are the most common languages, except French, but it is doubtful that at present any single language is understood by more than one tenth of the popultaion. The official language of the Ivory Coast is French and learning to read and write the language constitutes a major part of the young Ivorian's because Ivorians, especially the Agni and Baoulé, tend to consider menial work as being beneath their dignity. There are also large numbers of Malians, Ghanaians, Guineans,

Soccer, because of its universal popularity, is a factor in bringing together the Ivory Coast and other nations of the world.

33

An old mosque near the textile factory at Bouaké testifies to the prevalence of Islam in the northern Ivory Coast.

short stories such as Kaffi Atta, Charles Konan and Joseph Bognini Miezan.

B. Holas is the author of numerous works dealing with African, and particularly Ivorian, anthropology, art and culture. Among these are *L'Homme noir d'Afrique* (The Black Man of Africa), *Arts traditionnels de la Côte d'Ivoire* and *Les Senoufo*. A historian of note is Adiko Assoi, author of *Histoire des peuples noirs* (History of the Black Peoples).

RELIGION

Over 60 per cent of the population of the Ivory Coast practices animism, a compelling combination of traditional doctrine, ritual, and magic. In its simplest form, animism is the belief that all things of the world—even the inanimate ones—are infused with life and spirit. Thus animals, trees, rocks, and stars are said to possess souls.

In order to maintain peace and security in a natural world that is so infused with potentially harmful spirits it is necessary to pacify, venerate and occasionally seek the help of the various spirits. This is the job of the sorcerer or priest, who is invariably one of the most important members of the village.

Just as there is an abundance of different ethnic groups and languages in the Ivory Coast, so there are many different strains of animism. Usually the differences are simply a matter of emphasis.

The Baoulé and Akan peoples of the southeast place the greatest emphasis upon relations with the spirits of their ancestors. The crucial task of the priest is to maintain harmony between the living and the dead.

Among the southwest forest peoples, many tribes associate themselves with the spirit of a particular animal such as a buffalo, antelope, or elephant.

The secret societies of the Yacouba wield great magic power and are said to be able to become leopards at night, passing through the forest unnoticed, accomplishing tasks set out by the sorcerer.

Animism is especially popular in rural areas where people are not so heavily exposed to other religions. Rural Ivorians, because they

education. Because of the proximity of different ethnic groups and languages, Ivorians are slowly becoming multi-lingual.

LITERATURE

Ivorian literature in the French language began with a short comedy, *Les villes*, written in 1933 by Bernard Dadié. A later play by Dadié, *Assemien Dehle*, was produced in Paris in 1937 at the Théâtre des Champs-Elysées. Dadié has also written novels and short stories. Another leading writer is Amon d'Aby, who is not only a playwright but the author of serious studies of various aspects of Ivorian life. One of his best known plays is *Kwaa Adjoba*.

Other writers are the novelists Joba Aké and Maurice Koné, the poets Kanié Anoma and Bertin Gbohourou N'Guessan, and writers of

Muslims touch their head to the ground facing Mecca and engage in prayer during a religious celebration. About 24 per cent of Ivorians are Muslim.

lead simple lives and work so close to the earth, relate to the world in a reverential and spiritual manner.

The influence of animism is strong and pervasive. Because the religion is linked to a traditional view of the world, animism is exceedingly resistant to change. Even city dwellers, after becoming Muslim or Christian, are liable to resort to animist practices in special times of need.

ISLAM

Islam originated in 7th-century Arabia, when Allah (God) commanded his inspired prophet Mohammed to spread the doctrine of the Sacred Koran. Today, Islam is the second largest religion in the world—there are 125,000,000 Muslims in Africa alone.

Islam spread to West Africa in three waves. The Berbers brought the faith to the Ghanaian Empire in the 9th century A.D. From the 13th to the 18th centuries, the Malinke sovereigns spread Islam throughout the savannah region that defined the Mali Empire. The last wave occurred in the 19th century as the Malinke sovereign Samory Touré and his Muslim militia men roared across the savannahs inducing thousands of conversions through intimidation.

Muslims are quite numerous throughout the Ivory Coast, composing 24 per cent of the population. Part of the reason for the success of Islam in the Ivory Coast lies in the fact that the religion so readily provides a common ground, a measure of social integration to an otherwise disjointed assortment of ethnic groups. Furthermore, Islam is not usually at odds with animism. The religion neatly blends formal doctrine and magic in the person of the Marabout, a Muslim high priest who is invested with magical powers, healing, and fortune telling as well as with moral authority.

CHRISTIANITY

Christianity, which accounts for 14 per cent of the population, is most often found in the southern cities and tends to be the religion of the literate middle class and the elite. Unlike Islam, adherence to Christianity demands the sacrifice of traditional animist beliefs and is therefore viewed warily by rural Ivorians.

In 1914, Christianity in the Ivory Coast was given impetus by a prophet named William Wade Harris, who travelled along the lagoon-spotted coast preaching the word of God. The natives were attracted by his simple holy life and religious zeal, and over 120,000 of them were personally baptized by Harris.

Harrisism, which denounced witchcraft fetishes as evil, did much to weaken the hold of animism on southern Ivorians, and to spur the growth of Christianity in the country.

MUSIC AND DANCE

Music and dance are principal modes of expression for all Africans. All public functions in the Ivory Coast incorporate music. Singly and socially, in cities and in rural villages, Ivorians cause their country to vibrate with music.

When the occasion is ceremonial, the music is usually performed formally, strictly according

In the acrobatic and death-defying dance of the Guere, after various acrobatic stunts, the man will throw the young boy high into the air and pass sharp, glistening knives under his body as he descends. The dancers and the master of ceremony, usually the chief, always engage in prayer before the ritual dance, seeking the help and blessings of the spirits. Young boys, 4 to 5 years old, are recruited for the dance on the basis of their stamina and physical aptitude, and must undergo rigorous training before they can perform.

Ivorians get involved in their music.

36

This balafon player is from the northern region.

to pre-established form. However, most of the music resounding throughout the Ivory Coast is not ceremonial but rather social in nature.

There is no distinction between audience and performers. Everyone participates—humming, singing, clapping, hooting, or playing some instrument. The music is therefore very spontaneous, and a great deal of improvisation occurs.

The drum is the universally understood and approved instrument in Africa. The Ivory Coast has drums of all sizes and shapes. Drumming is considered a fine art among some groups, and masters develop rhythms that are stunning in their complexity. Another traditional Ivorian instrument is a wooden xylophone called a *balafon*. It is common in the north, especially among the Senoufo.

In the coastal cities of West Africa, creative musicians have successfully blended traditional rhythms and American soul music to form a new, distinctive and exciting style of music that is tremendously popular among Ivorian youth. Afrobeat, as the new music is called, incorporates electric guitars, saxophones, horns and a variety of percussion instruments.

While dancing, too, is often a spontaneous social activity, the most outstanding dances of

The "temate" is a dance of the region of Man— traditionally performed by young girls during the rice harvest.

Ivorian arts and crafts are produced quickly and in great number by the government's flourishing crafts industry, but still retain the dynamism of original antique masks and statues.

the Ivory Coast occur in conjunction with established ceremonies and events. Many ceremonial dances are quite theatrical, involving elaborate and vivid costumes and masks. The dances of the region of Man emphasize acrobatic manoeuvres and potentially dangerous stunts.

ARTS AND CRAFTS

The Ivory Coast has long been renowned for the quality of its art including some of the most technically competent wood-carving in all of Africa. Originally Ivorian art objects were most commonly masks or statues created for ceremonial occasions. Today, the objects are produced in greater number for sale to tourists and collectors.

For each group, art objects are created within the prescribed traditional patterns of their culture. Therefore, the art object is more the expression of the culture than the individual.

The Baoulé, as a culture, are especially artistically inclined. They are one of the few groups that produce artwork not only for ceremony but also for the simple satisfaction of aesthetic expression. Baoulé homes are often graced by carved doors and furniture and numerous decorative objects.

The statues and masks of the Senoufo often combine human or animal features in a weird, nightmarish fashion. The style evolved by the

Senoufo, however grotesque, is considered one of the most important contributions to African art.

A shoemaker makes sandals in the African quarter of Treichville, Abidjan.

38

Woman in Bondage is the subject of this carving. The Ivory Coast is one of the most prolific wood-carving countries in Africa.

Modern arts such as professional theatre, cinematography, and literature, are at an early stage of development in the Ivory Coast and at this point do not constitute a significant element in the life of most Ivorians.

EDUCATION

The average Ivorian child will experience two forms of education—traditional and modern.

Traditional education begins at birth and is a continuing process of teaching the child the traditions and mores of his society. The climax of the traditional education occurs at puberty when the adolescent, during a moving, sometimes frightening ceremony, is initiated into manhood or womanhood.

The formal educational system of the Ivory Coast is strictly patterned after that of the French. Some Ivorians believe that the French educational standards are too high for them, given their traditional background.

Besides wood-carving and sculpture, the peoples of the Ivory Coast engage extensively in pottery, painting, and goldsmithing.

At the Teacher Training Institute in Abidjan, a student listens to tapes in the language laboratory.

39

The television production studios at Bouaké are used primarily to transmit educational broadcasts.

Many Ivorian students have trouble in assimilating the French language. About one-half of those who begin primary school (at 6 years) will complete it.

The small number who do complete primary school, and continue through secondary school and perhaps university, are liable to become mentally and spiritually removed from their people due to the extensive exposure to French manners and customs.

Efforts are being made by the government to expand the educational system and to bring it more closely in tune with the needs, abilities and culture of Ivorians.

Future science teachers study physics in this laboratory in Abidjan's Teacher Training Institute.

Using the latest equipment, Abidjan housewives learn modern techniques in an up-to-date cooking class.

A French expert instructs an Ivorian student in the operation of the central Telex of the Société de Telecommunications Africaine in Abidjan.

HEALTH

While public health in the Ivory Coast compares well with that of nearby countries, it is still depressingly low by American or European standards. Overcrowding, inadequate water and sewage facilities, and a lack of health education, all combine to create a widespread sanitation problem that is the major obstacle to public health.

In extremely poor areas, especially the northern savannah region, nutritional deficiencies contribute to poor health. The agrarian Ivorians of this region live mainly on millet and rice, and are therefore lacking essential protein and vitamins in their diet.

With poor sanitation and nutritional deficiencies so widespread, Ivorians are especially susceptible to disease and many of them succumb each year to malaria and other parasitic diseases, and to yaws, pneumonia and tuber-

41

This antiseptically clean, modern operating room is part of the Hospital Center of Cocody, one of the finest medical facilities in all of Africa.

culosis. The average life expectancy is about 40 years.

Steps are being taken by the Ministry of Public Health and Population, which supervises all medical service in the country, to raise the standard of public health.

The Ministry has two major problems—to reach and provide health care to outlying, isolated territories and to break down the distrust the natives have for modern medicine.

All health care is free in the Ivory Coast. The Ministry has brought endemic diseases, such as smallpox and yellow fever, under control by providing mass vaccinations. Modern hospitals have been established in Abidjan and Bouaké and mobile units spread health education and treatment to the outlying areas.

FOOD

Staple foods in the Ivory Coast include yams, plantains (which are like large green bananas), rice, millet and groundnuts (peanuts). The emphasis on these foods varies in different places. In the northern savannah region, rice

with a peppery peanut sauce is an omnipresent dish. Closer to the coast, fish served with fried plantains is popular.

Lunchtime at the Plateau market—the women are selling foutou, rice with fish sauce, ragoût, and other typical Ivorian dishes.

42

Throughout the southern Ivory Coast you will find women on street corners roasting large cooking bananas called plantains. These tasty snacks are quite filling and cost only a penny or two.

At Abobo-Baoula, near Abidjan, a cheerful cook prepares a hot meal for the children of an elementary school.

Produce is sold in a spacious, airy market on the outskirts of Abidjan.

However, *foutou*, the national dish of the Ivory Coast, is made by pounding plantains or yams in a mortar to form a sticky dough, and is then served with a highly seasoned meat sauce. Foutou is eaten by hand and the process of securing a fingerful of dough, dipping it in the sauce and popping it into one's mouth can be embarrassing for a beginner. Bush rats and large snails are sometimes eaten in the forested regions.

The abundance of fresh food and vegetables in the Ivory Coast make every market-place a bright-hued scene. The pineapples of the Ivory Coast are sweet and juicy, and together with the bananas, mangoes, papayas, and oranges, they enrich and lend variety to the Ivorian diet.

This hardy root is called manioc, or cassava. Manioc is a staple food in the northern region and is grown chiefly around Bouaké, Korhogo, and Man. The roots are mashed to form a rice-like substance which is then served wrapped in a palm leaf.

44

Even the youngest child can carry a basin of fish on his head.

Wherever you find ribbons hanging in the doorway, there also you find an African eating establishment. This particular restaurant in Yamoussoukro is renowned for its excellent preparation of an Ivorian delicacy that consists of a large bush rat stewed with vegetables and seasonings.

With an annual catch of 45,000 tons, the fishing industry in the Ivory Coast is helping to put the country on the road to self-sufficiency. Some 30,000 tons are smoked for local use. Here, workmen proceed with a step in the smoking process.

The Plateau district of Abidjan is the commercial hub of the country, with high-rise office buildings housing international businesses. The bustling metropolis falls silent at night, as working people return to their respective suburbs.

5. ECONOMY

THE IVORY COAST is being spurred towards progress by one of the fastest growing and most energetic economies in Africa. The gross national product almost quadrupled between 1960 and 1975. The per capita income is U.S. $300 per year, one of the highest in Africa.

This remarkable economic growth has resulted from an expansion of agriculture and improvement in agricultural methods and equipment, development of the forestry industry, and a dramatic "take-off" in Ivorian export industries.

The present economy of the Ivory Coast is the result of long-range planning by President Houphouët-Boigny and his advisors. When Boigny became president in 1960, the Ivory Coast was blessed with many potentially valuable natural resources, but very little income. Most major financial transactions occurred with France. Boigny realized that in order to attract the money necessary to stimulate the Ivorian economy, he must create a good investment climate. A liberal capitalism developed, with tax exemptions, no restrictions on repa-

These cattle and their guides seem in no hurry. Animal husbandry is a weak link in the economy of the Ivory Coast—about 80 per cent of the meat consumed in the country is imported.

triation of profits, and a governmental attitude that sought to ensure profit for investors. Boigny channelled the foreign money that first trickled, then poured, into the Ivory Coast into agriculture, the most basic sector of the economy.

AGRICULTURE

Agriculture is the backbone of the economy and the livelihood of most Ivorians. Agriculture accounts for 83 per cent of the exports of the Ivory Coast. The economic success in agriculture is due in part to the deep-water port at Abidjan and the well developed network of roads that make it easy to transport products quickly to African markets and to other parts of the world.

Two major crops, coffee and cocoa, account for 55 per cent of the total exports. The Ivory Coast in 1976 was the world's third largest producer of both coffee and cocoa, and the

Members of La Fraternelle Co-operative in Abidjan build a cottage.

Workers pound earth with heavy mallets to build a water-catchment dam near Bouaké, in order to conserve water for the dry season. The geese in the background will benefit from this, since the site of the dam is a poultry farm.

These men are not building a levee—they are simply stacking bags at the Grands Moulins flour mill in Abidjan, one of the largest in Africa.

Cultivation of rubber occurs mainly in the Southwest. The Ivorian rubber industry receives technical assistance from French and United States companies.

world's fourth largest producer of pineapples, which only began to be cultivated seriously in 1950. The Ivory Coast is the leading producer of bananas in Africa, and was sixth in the world in 1976.

President Houphouët-Boigny realized early the importance of diversifying agriculture. If the economy depends too heavily on two or three export crops, it will suffer severe setbacks when international market prices fall. Therefore, a scheme of diversification was begun in 1962. New experimental crops were raised, some of which have come to flourish in recent years.

Palm oil, which has long been an essential ingredient in the preparation of African food, was originally secured from wild palm trees for local use. In the early 1960's the trees began to be cultivated for export, and in 1974, the Ivory Coast was the world's leading exporter of this product.

The cultivation of rubber trees, which began on a small scale in 1956, continued to grow through the 1960's and is now beginning to pay dividends. Two new large plantations are being established in the southwest, financed by international banks and under the technical supervision of the Michelin (France) and Goodyear (United States) companies.

Cotton had been cultivated haphazardly and on a small scale since 1930, but production skyrocketed in 1960 with the introduction of

The yam harvest is a festive occasion in some parts of the Ivory Coast. Yams, an Ivorian staple, may weigh as much as 100 pounds (45 kilos).

Cotton plantations are found in the north and central parts of the Ivory Coast. While cotton is not a major crop and total production is low compared to major African producers, the plantations have contributed greatly to the economy by supplying Ivorian textile concerns.

new growing methods. Much of the raw cotton supplies the Ivory Coast's own textile mills.

Other export crops currently being developed are coconuts, rice, sugar cane and tobacco.

FORESTRY

The southern half of the Ivory Coast is covered with more than 12,000,000 acres (4,800,000 hectares) of thick forest. While the timber industry began slowly with the export

The southern forest region of the Ivory Coast provides the ideal growing conditions for cocoa—shade, ample rainfall, and protection from the wind. During the harvest, the pods are cut down with a machete and broken open. Then the cocoa beans are extracted, fermented, and finally dried in the sun. Note that the fruit grows directly from the trunk.

of mahogany, the strength of the industry grew as new usable species were discovered and exploited. Recently, timber has surpassed coffee as the principal export.

To process the natural abundance of timber, the Ivory Coast has a growing number of sawmills and other wood-processing operations producing plywood, veneers, crates, boxes, cabinets and furniture.

The entire forestry industry is strictly regulated by the Waters and Forest Service of the National Government, whose primary objective is the conservation and growth of forest reserves.

A worker waters a vegetable plot at an experimental farm.

Timber has recently surpassed coffee as the number one export of the Ivory Coast. Rather than shipping raw timber abroad, the government seeks to develop local wood-processing industries such as sawmills and carpentry shops. The government is encouraging Ivorians to become financially involved in the timber industry by granting tax concessions to investors.

Workers operate sewing machines in a textile factory at Bouaké.

INDUSTRY

In order to expand the economic base, and to become more self-sufficient, the Ivory Coast, with help from foreign investors, has poured considerable energy and money into various domestic and export industries.

For domestic use, there are factories, located mainly in Abidjan and Bouaké, that process and package milk products, soda, cigarettes, matches, soap and many other everyday items. There are automobile and radio factories in Bouaké.

One of the most important new export industries, in terms of reducing regional economic disparities, is the sugar refinery being established in the relatively poor savannah region in the north. The refinery, situated in Ferkessédougou, is being built with United States money and technical support, and will eventually have an output capacity of 60,000 tons (54,000 tonnes) per year.

Plans are also being made for a sackcloth factory in Ferkesssédougou, a cotton grain mill in Bouaké, a textile company in Agboville, and a ready-made clothing industry near Abidjan. A new, expensive textile industry will be built in Gonfreville, near Bouaké, which already houses the oldest textile concern in the country.

This checkered cloth is being produced at the textile factory in Gonfreville, near Bouaké. The textile industry is presently being geared towards exportation and two new plants are planned for Bouaké and Agboville.

The single oil refinery in the Ivory Coast is located on the Vridi canal, just across the lagoon from the Plateau in Abidjan. The refinery, which came into service in 1965, produces gasoline, oil, kerosene and diesel fuel.

This factory in Bouaké processes Ivorian tobacco for cigarettes. The government is promoting such light industries enthusiastically, in an effort to expand the economic base of the country.

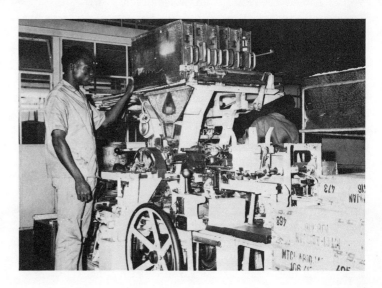

Dedicated in November, 1972, the new Kossou dam is almost a mile (1.6 km.) long and 200 ft. (60 metres) high. The dam, which crosses the River Bandama near Yamoussoukro, flooded a large area, necessitating the relocation of 75,000 residents. The villagers did not object to the population transfer because they realized the huge benefits the project would bring.

THE GRAND PROJECTS

As part of its long-range economic plan, the Ivory Coast has been engaged in two ambitious projects of great social and economic importance.

The first project was the construction of the Kossou dam near Yamoussoukro. The cost of the project was U.S. $170,000,000, three fourths of which was spent on the actual construction of the dam. The remainder was used to effect the transfer of 75,000 people that was necessary when the water level rose. At peak efficiency, the dam produces 500,000,000 kilowatts, which equals the power production of the entire country.

One positive side effect of the project is that high yield coffee, cocoa, and rice crops are made possible by irrigating large expanses of land. Also promising to add to the growth of the areas is the man-made lake at Kossou which will eventually become a tourist hub offering first-class accommodations and all types of water sports.

Operation San Pedro is a three-pronged development plan that will dramatically change the southwestern Ivory Coast. The project includes the construction of a deep-water port capable of handling large freighters and liners, the erection of a town providing housing and facilities for 25,000 inhabitants and a 300-mile (480-km.) road network connecting Daloa to the new coastal town at San Pedro.

Operation San Pedro will cost about U.S. $58,000,000 and is being financed by the Ivory Coast, Italy, France and Germany. By improving communication and land and sea transportation, Operation San Pedro will make possible the exploitation of agriculture and forestry resources that had hitherto been neglected.

Workers at Gagoulai, in the southwest, secure a new piece of pipe to the shaft of a drilling rig, as part of a geologic survey.

Urban workers account for only a small part of the Ivory Coast's manpower. Unlike this dock worker, nearly 90 per cent of the people are engaged in such pursuits as farming, fishing, stock-raising and forestry.

The deep-water port at San Pedro is nearing completion. Operation San Pedro, which involves the creation of a port, a town, and a system of roads in the densely forested southwest, will skyrocket the timber industry.

People dislocated by the building of the Kossou dam have been resettled, with United Nations help, in 70 new villages like this one.

TOURISM

The tourism industry, because it is non-agricultural and therefore not as susceptible to fluctuations in the international market, is being energetically stimulated by the government of the Ivory Coast.

The elegant, 750-room Hotel Ivoire in Abidjan, with seven restaurants, swimming pools, a casino, a golf course, and even an ice-skating

This is the beginning of the African Riviera project, a daring experiment in tourism and urban planning.

The surfside holiday village at Assinie is run by the Club Méditerranée, an international tourist organization.

rink, is an example of the enthusiasm with which the government pursues this economic endeavor.

The government has joined numerous private investors in creating the Ivorian Company for Tourism and Hotel Trade. This organization has established a network of fine hotels throughout the Ivory Coast.

Highlights of the tourism industry in the Ivory Coast are the two elaborate seaside resorts that have been established in the last few years at Assinie and Assouinde, to the east of Abidjan.

But the grandest and most ambitious experiment in tourism in the history of West Africa is the "African Riviera" that will occupy 10,000 acres (4,000 hectares) of lagoonal coast to the east of Abidjan. The project involves the construction of a garden city of 120,000 inhabitants, an international exhibition complex, plush and varied accommodations and entertainment facilities, a Disneyland-type amusement park, and an animal reserve.

TRANSPORTATION

The Ivory Coast has one of the best developed road networks in West Africa. In 1971, there were 21,875 miles (35,000 km.) of road, 10,310

The Hotel Ivoire towers over the city of Abidjan, symbolizing the grandness of the Ivorian economic plan. The hotel has 750 rooms and every conceivable luxury for the international traveller.

Passengers crowd aboard a train at a stop between Abidjan and Bouaké.

OUTLOOK

While the burgeoning economy of the Ivory Coast has greatly enhanced the quality of life of some citizens, it has also, inevitably, created some problems.

There is a gross financial inequality in the Ivory Coast, with a very small percentage of the population, mostly European, controlling much of the spendable income. Top management positions in business and industry are usually filled by Europeans, and many Ivorians are understandably annoyed.

Since 1962, President Houphouët-Boigny has advocated and effected a policy of Ivorization—the process of bringing the fiscal and

miles (16,496 km.) of which are usable all year round. Privately owned buses transport Ivorians between cities.

The Abidjan-Niger Railway runs right down the middle of the Ivory Coast, covering the 700-mile (1,120-km.) stretch between Abidjan and Ouaga, Upper Volta.

A host of international airlines service the Ivory Coast through Abidjan's Port Bouét airport, which is fully equipped to handle jet traffic. Nine other airports are situated across the Ivory Coast and are serviced by the national airlines, Air Ivoire.

The port of Abidjan is the largest in French-speaking Africa. There are 14 wharves for docking, loading, storage and other port functions as well as extensive warehouse facilities. The port accommodates international passenger liners and freighters.

Backpacking is the chief form of infant travel in the Ivory Coast. Women are able to carrry on all sorts of activity with their offspring so attached, and hardly a complaint is heard from the little ones, who are usually sleeping.

A United Nations fish-processing expert inspects local methods of smoking fish.

industrial management of the Ivory Coast into the hands of Ivorians. The President feels that Ivorization is essential, but that it must be accomplished gradually, never at the risk of competence or growth.

To this end, the government has subsidized the training of Ivorians for high-level positions and has lent financial aid to Ivorian entrepreneurs. In 1972, non-Ivorian professionals such as doctors and lawyers were forbidden to open new practices.

Another different sort of problem results

A specialist analyzes copper samples from the southwest Ivory Coast.

Fishermen work on their nets at Abidjan.

Fish is a prime source of protein in the Ivorian diet. While the fishing industry has grown steadily in recent years, the Ivory Coast must still import a great deal of fish. Efforts are being made to develop the industry to the point where it will be able to fulfill domestic needs.

Geological studies are in progress in many parts of the Ivory Coast in a search for new mineral resources. Here a technician operates a spectrogram in a mineralogy laboratory in Abidjan.

from the accelerated urbanization process that the society is going through. Abidjan grew from 180,000 in 1960 to over 600,000 in 1976.

Rapid urbanization has led to unemployment, housing, welfare and crime problems. Perhaps the most serious problem is the loss of traditional values that accompany the shift from the village to the crowded, impersonal economics-oriented city.

The family—that social institution around which traditional life revolved—is undergoing severe stress as increasing numbers of young people leave their villages for the city.

These problems all derive from a larger dilemma, one that is common to all developing African countries. It is the conflict between the old and the new, between traditional values and modern values, and every Ivorian must somehow reconcile the two if he is to lead a productive and psychologically secure life.

INDEX